DAILY EXPRESS and SUNDAY EXPRESS
Cartoons
Fifty Sixth Series

Giles characters™ and © 2004 Express Newspapers

Published By Express Newspapers, 10 Lower Thames Street, London EC3R 6AE

ISBN 0-85079-301-7

An Introduction by

Alan Titchmarsh

The Giles Annual appeared in my father's Christmas stocking every year when I was a nipper and after he had read it from cover to cover I would settle down with it in front of a roaring fire.

I suppose I would have been ten or eleven when I really began to appreciate the sharp topicality of Giles's humour but long before that I had learned to love his drawings because I knew two of his characters 'intimately'. Grandma was just like my grandma and Vera was a dead ringer for my Auntie Alice. Like Giles's cartoon characters they lived - and bickered - together in a tiny terrace house. I can only think that Giles must have bumped into my relatives in their home town of Ilkley, Yorkshire at some point - how else could he have captured them so well? Oh and then there was 'Chalky' the schoolmaster who I'm convinced was modelled on our local verger.

I still remember every detail in Giles's cartoons. One in particular depicted a farmer at the Smithfield Show trying to board an overflowing double-decker bus at the end of the day. 'I'll have to get on', he explained to the conductor. 'Me Aberdeen Angus be gorn upstairs'. Why that particular one should remain lodged in my mind I've no idea except that it struck me as being very funny.

Giles's cartoons are timeless - even when they portray historic events. Now I'm not sure if that's a contradiction but what I do know is that they still make me smile and all these years later I remain lost in admiration for the man's mastery of his craft.

ALAN TITCHMARSH MBE VMH

"Leave the doors open, Harry."

Daily Express, August 27th, 1963

"I'll go and get you a plate of little frogs' legs to cheer you up."

Daily Express, September 3rd, 1963

"We'll have to stop him breaking these speed records before breakfast."

Daily Express, September 3rd, 1981

"Now that we've got over our first day at school I think we'll get down to a few mutual understandings, like me doing the driving, and you all sitting very, very still."

Daily Express, September 5th, 1967

"I believe mine is glad we're going back to school too – he's been singing Glory Hallelujah ever since he got up."

Daily Express, September 7th, 1965

"Here we are Vera, 'Last date for posting Christmas cards overland to Zambia, Barindi, Chile, Rwanda and Uganda – Monday.'"

Daily Express, September 10th, 1981

"As senior executive of the accounts department, under no circumstances whatsoever will I sit on your lap."

Daily Express, September 11th, 1975

"Harry was only whistling 'All things bright and beautiful' when over comes this vicar and dings him a beaut."

Sunday Express, September 13th, 1964

"I don't know why she's 'ollering. She's never sent a letter with a stamp on it yet."

Sunday Express, September 15th, 1968

"The Home Secretary says my lapse into crime may be because the threat of nuclear war
has made me disillusioned and undermined my morals."

Sunday Express, September 22nd, 1963

"As the Bank Rate's been cut ½% may I suggest that this week you put something in instead of whipping something out."

Sunday Express, September 22nd, 1968

"All my life I've listened to talk about the 'Good old days'. The way things are going I reckon we're going to get a chance to sample them."

Daily Express, September 23rd, 1982

"It's a summons from a burglar who broke in and stole half a bottle of Grandma's home-made wine and has never been the same since."

Sunday Express, September 26th, 1982

"Hold it right there! Will the brighter pupil inform the less-bright pupils of an antidote to his latest concoction?"

Daily Express, September 28th, 1978

"I've asked you in the nicest possible way already – please do not sweep another load of haddock heads under my barrow."

Daily Express, September 29th, 1970

"Sounds good, don't it? 'My dearest Lucinda, Can't get away to marry you today as I'm cleaning out Battersea Sewage Station'."

Sunday Express, October 4th, 1970

"He found Skegness so bracing he's decided to come back to stay with his family."
(Visiting walrus returned to Arctic from Skegness.)

Sunday Express, October 4th, 1981

One way to beat the breathalyser next week will be to share the driving home between you. One do the driving on—

Monday . . .

One on Tuesday . . .

One on Wednesday . . .

One on Thursday . . .

One on Friday . . .

And so on.

Daily Express, October 6th, 1967

"I know they all had Chi-Chi to take their minds off the Labour Conference – but I'm not letting Goldie out to take their minds off yours."

Sunday Express, October 9th, 1966

"With a bit of luck we'll lose him in this fog then WHOOSH! away it goes."
(The dustmen's strike spreads.)

Sunday Express, October 12th, 1969

"And may I ask what you want seats that recline into a double bed as an optional extra for?"

Daily Express, October 17th, 1974

"I've had a word with the lady, Vicar. She's not collecting for the Church Restoration Fund, she's collecting for Grandma's Day."

Sunday Express, October 20th, 1974

"One small modification of the rules – no one goes over the wall to get their ball back."

Sunday Express, October 21st, 1979

"FLORRIE, we've got a blackleg at number 132."

Daily Express, October 24th, 1969

"The ref's blown for offside – you can tell by the bubbles."

Sunday Express, October 24th, 1982

"Forget it!"

Daily Express, October 29th, 1964

"Gently, copper – lay even yer little finger on me and I could probably get yer a month for assault."

Daily Express, October 31st, 1952

"Poor little devils – they can just afford the BR cheaper food, but they can't afford the dearer fares."

Daily Express, October 31st, 1978

"I'm for the way the Russians choose their presidents – quick and quiet."

Daily Express, November 3rd, 1964

"RIGHT! All those who switched on their heaters this morning, fall out."

Daily Express, November 3rd, 1966

"Dad, there's a man at the door with a petition for the abolition of domestic pets. No there isn't."

Sunday Express, November 3rd, 1974

"We demand police protection from independent bodies taking pictures of us at work."
(Gang captured by secret camera.)

Daily Express, November 10th, 1981

"Your wife's in the bar, Harry. I explained you were our keenest member
or you wouldn't be playing 18 holes in the fog."

Sunday Express, November 16th, 1975

"If you'd read Egon Ronay's report on airport meals, you'd know those little hard things on your x-ray are not concealed bullets – they're called 'Fresh English garden peas'."

Daily Express, November 19th, 1974

"Morning, Froid – we hear you're the only boy who did his homework instead of watching football last night."

Daily Express, November 19th, 1981

The first thing you'll get if they enforce longer hours for shopworkers will be a slight fall in the standard of service.

Daily Express, November 20th, 1952

"Cissies."

Sunday Express, November 24th, 1963

"One thing for sure, Buttercup – no one can accuse a cattle market of looking like a beauty contest."

Daily Express, November 24th, 1970

"I sometimes have doubts about some of ours, Mac. Grave doubts."

Daily Express, November 26th, 1970

NOVEMBER MORN...
"Right! Open ranks. Girls on one side of the footpath, boys the other."

Daily Express, November 28th, 1968

"Good evening, Mrs Sykes. I'm searching for a member of my flock who hath gone astray – a rather well-fed turkey, to be precise."

Sunday Express, November 29th, 1981

"Same as last year, sir – Lads' Club Choral Society accusing the Choir of opening the carol season on their pitch."

Daily Express, December 4th, 1952

"I've written and told the Express the only way they can solve my Christmas present problem is by sending me a cheque."

Daily Express, December 4th, 1975

"I know another member of the environment they want to arm – the Christmas fairy in Santa's Grotto at Harridges."

Daily Express, December 4th, 1980

"Mum, quick! Dad's on television!"

Daily Express, December 5th, 1978

"Over to you, Miss Markham – and the very best of luck."

Sunday Express, December 7th, 1952

"Not only is it no longer legal to make a run for home, Sir, it seems you've picked the wrong house."

Sunday Express, December 7th, 1969

"Christmas comes but once a year – another fort for me and another doll's cradle for you."

Sunday Express, December 8th, 1985

"Having to take the kids with 'em this year is going to cramp their style a bit up West."

Daily Express, December 9th, 1969

"Good Christian men, re-joy-oy-ace – and keep your eye on Smithy in this blinking fog."

Sunday Express, December 13th, 1964

"Now who do you think has come all the way across the country to cheer you up?"

Sunday Express, December 15th, 1974

"Doris! You didn't tell me you'd taken a part-time job for Christmas."

Daily Express, December 16th, 1982

"Now this merry festive death-ray gun, Madam, lets out a stream of devastating nerve gas which disintegrates any living object within range. And boy, do I wish it did!"

Daily Express, December 17th, 1970

THE BARONESS ILLUSTRATED... (six of one and half a dozen of the other)

Daily Express, December 19th, 1968

"It's your fault – you said let's buy Grandma some tights for Christmas for a joke."

Sunday Express, December 20th, 1964

"I told the Vicar we intend to strike on Christmas Eve when it'll hurt most
and he said the way we have been singing lately it was a good idea."

Sunday Express, December 20th, 1970

"Your Yuletide message to the office party last year, sir? Same as the year before – Merry Christmas, everybody. Over and out."

Daily Express, December 20th, 1979

"How come a Great Dane bit a Crown Court Judge and got off with a pat on the head, yet Butch gets porridge for eating a couple of Grandma's Christmas Cards?"

Sunday Express, December 21st, 1975

"You've bought Grandma a WHAT for Christmas?"

Sunday Express, December 21st, 1980

"Rejoice good Christian men – the group's arrived."

Daily Express, December 24th, 1981

"Come, come – SOME of us must be telling little fibs."

Scottish Sunday Express, December 25th, 1966

"Stop making holly wreaths, everybody – he's up."

Sunday Express, December 28th, 1952

"One person who's not going to think much of it – my Auntie Bertha – that's certain."

Daily Express, December 29th, 1964

"Why don't you take the aunts for a nice walk while we get the lunch?"

Sunday Express, December 29th, 1985

"Don't fly off the handle, Grandma – we're only using your bed while our
Christmas present's got flu."

Daily Express, December 30th, 1969

"Don't shove, Mary – I want to get back to work as much as you want me to!"

Daily Express, December 31st, 1985

"He said 'Happy New Year' to everyone we met and when they'd gone a little way past he said 'and I hope you fall down a hole.'"

Daily Express, January 1st, 1953

"Your Dad's New Year resolution – jogging. He only got to the end of the road where the police found him in a 'distressed condition' – could you go and pick him up?"

Daily Express, January 2nd, 1986

"Madam, because there happens to be nobody aboard, it does not mean this ship is abandoned, and what you have there is not salvage – it's loot."

Daily Express, January 6th, 1983

"In the event of power cuts watch out for Lover Boy in the corner."

Daily Express, January 10th, 1963

"Bennett, after diligent research into history, comes up with the illuminating observation that we have gone through 13 Prime Ministers since the birth of Donald Duck."

Daily Express, January 10th, 1980

Way up among the major crisis stories of the week comes the recommendation by a Royal Society
that it is safer for mothers to PULL their prams across the road instead of PUSHING.

Daily Express, January 12th, 1967

BACK TO SCHOOL WEEK –
by BRITAIN'S MOST FAMOUS CARTOONIST

"Back to School" for me would not mean back to one of your modern rest homes for unretired infants where the children run the teachers.

It would be back to one of the old-fashioned schools that I went to where the teachers ran the children.

Or thought they did.

Back to one of those grey brick boxes on asphalt, where the only useful thing you learned was the art of self-defence during short periods between lessons misnamed "playtime."

"Playtime" took place twice a day. Bang went a bell and out poured hundreds of small boys like a stream of black treacle, the bigger ones lamming into the smaller ones and the smaller ones lamming into the very small ones.

Another bang on the bell announced "playtime" over, and back you all poured into the grey brick box where everybody except the very, very good ones got lammed by the teachers.

When the teachers grew tired of lamming they used the very, very good ones as examples for showing the bad ones up.

COLLABORATORS

We never seemed able to lay hands on these very, very good ones during playtime because they were always missing.

It has occurred to me since that those who were not creeping about the grey brick box collaborating with the teachers as monitors and prefects were probably using the far corner of the playground as a

Daily Express, January 13th, 1953

safety-zone, where they stayed hidden until the end-of-playtime bell gave them the all-clear.

If I went back to school now I should pay more attention to these fifth columnists.

As far as the so-called lessons were concerned, in a class of 50-odd fellow-candidates for delinquency, I expect I should still come out somewhere near the bottom of the exam sheet.

Lessons were instilled into you both ends—by whacking your ear or caning the part you sit down with. They included things like history, geography, art, singing, sums, and most of the accumulated nonsense of the past, with very little reference to the future.

You were reminded every morning about the importance of punctuality by two on each for being late. It was so nice when I left school not to be caned for being late that I have been late ever since.

THOSE DATES !

History meant remembering the dates of battles of the last two thousand years. As I still can't remember the dates of battles for the last two weeks I should still flop at History.

Geography was the names of rivers and volcanoes. I know no more now about (a) rivers and (b) volcanoes than I knew then, except (a) the river that starts at the bottom of my garden and (b) Lord Beaverbrook.

Art. Now there was a subject on which my teachers really used to let themselves go. They gave us a unique variety of things to draw, a cone, a cube, or the eternal green vase which stood next to the tadpole tank on the window sill of every classroom.

Daily Express, January 13th, 1953

None of this "Draw what you like" business. The first thing I should organise if I went back to school would be a campaign against all green vases.

Sums. My accountant will tell you that they couldn't have taught me very much about sums. I would still call mental arithmetic brain fever.

Singing. If I thought I should have to suffer another dose of our singing lessons I wouldn't go back.

'IF MR. GILES . . .'

The only information we got about the future was to be told how bad it was going to be if we got our name in the punishment book many more times.

But I could go back now armed with the knowledge that they were misinforming us on this count, for I have discovered since that nothing they forecast turned out to be anything like as bad as it is.

Perhaps the only sensible thing they tried to teach us was that it is wrong to smoke.

At 3s. 7d. for 20 they were dead right.

I could tell them they were quite wrong in chastising us for occasionally tarring and feathering the weaker fellow pupil, such things being looked upon nowadays as "self-expression."

Having read enough Hemingway and Dr. Kinsey to know most of the answers, I should know how to come back at that sarcastic old tyrant who lorded it over us for a couple of terms.

When he addressed me with his "If Mr. Giles would kindly come to the front of the class, place the gob-stopper he is sucking in the waste-paper basket, and hand me that intriguing piece of literature he is composing under his desk, I shall be delighted to read it aloud to the rest of the class while he goes upstairs and fetches the cane and book."

Knowing what I know now, I should just sit back and wait for the roar of laughter from my associate scholars to subside and then reply in the modern fashion, without removing my gob-stopper:—

"And if my clever substitute for a teacher doesn't watch his step he will leave me no option but to report him to the education committee and have him flung out on his ear."

It would be interesting to see how the old tyrant reacted to this treatment. I've a pretty good idea.

MY SYMPATHY

But, apart from the fact that I know I could make it a lot hotter for them now, I don't want to go back.

And lest the teachers of today should think me a trifle biased on the side of the pupils, I hasten to say they all have my deepest sympathy.

Strange as their methods were for passing on the wisdom of the universe, I wouldn't have fancied their chances of coping with the scholars in my part of the world had they not been armed by the authorities with canes, T-squares, bits of chalk to throw at us, and an ability to detect and stamp out any sign of originality before it got serious.

Next: I'm coming over to join the enemy by presenting on the following pages an Alphabetical Guide for Teachers. You needn't buy the paper unless you want to.

A for APPLE
offered to teacher.

B for BOYS
which boys will be.

C for CHILDREN.
Most adults think
all children are
lovely. Even the
fact that people
like Hitler were
one of these once
fails to shake their
faith in this popu-
lar misconception.

D for DRAWING
PINS. Used for
most things except
drawings.

E for ELASTIC.

F for FAWKES.
You taught 'em
about him.

G for "GOOD"
TYPE. What every
decent type tries
not to be.

H for HERO.

I for IF I were a
teacher I'd get
another job.

J for JOY. Ex-
pression registered
by scholars when
you fall over.

K for KEMISTRY.
See SMELLS.

L for LITERA-
TURE.

M for MOTHERS.
"Do I understand
you 'it my boy?"

N for NASTY
TYPE. Never
looks or smells
very fresh. Every
class has one.

Daily Express, January 15th, 1953

OVER TO THE ENEMY

 O for ORGANIS-ING TYPES. Responsible for nearly all class-room disorders.

 P for PAYOFF. The result of all your hard work.

 Q for QUIET SORT. Never risk turning your back on these.

 R for RUMBLE. Comes from the back of the room when the class is at its quietest.

 S for SMELLS. Carbide in your inkwell can account for one of these.

 T for TEAM SPIRIT.

 U for UNIFORMS.

 V for VASE. See this page last Tuesday.

 W for WOOD-WORK.

 X for WRONG.

 Y for YOU. How your pupils see you — and how you think they do.

 Z for ZINC. There's the zinc and the zoap. Get cracking.

 ✓ for RIGHT.

Daily Express, January 15th, 1953

"Progress is the realisation of Utopias." (Oscar Wilde)

Daily Express, January 14th, 1964

"That one makes me nervous. If she's still paying me full price for her cigarettes she must be having me on something else."

Daily Express, January 17th, 1967

"I told him as there's no football he can stay at home and amuse the children."

Sunday Express, January 20th, 1963

"We've got to sign an agreement that in the event of a future water shortage no way will they have to share a bath with Grandma."

Sunday Express, January 23rd, 1983

"I do not intend to disclose my source of information, but I have learned that you are all going to say you stayed away yesterday because your roads were blocked when in fact they were not."

Daily Express, January 24th, 1963

"Do you know what I think is wrong with those figures, Copper? They should be the other way round, that's what I think."

Sunday Express, January 24th, 1965

"I can't tell you exactly where you are, lady, but if you stop on that road and about thirty of them hit you up the rear you'll know you're on a motorway in England."

Daily Express, January 29th, 1970

"Come and have a look at one of the bloodthirsty hunting junkies – as Spike Milligan calls 'em."

Daily Express, February 2nd, 1982

"They've read about that post office cat who scared off those raiders."

Daily Express, February 5th, 1981

"Advice to the Modern Girl – at the first sound of the word GOLF hand back his ring."

Sunday Express, February 9th, 1969

"The Supreme Champion of this house has just eaten one of Auntie Ivy's shoes."

Sunday Express, February 9th, 1975

"Your Alfie's measles are certainly very much better since you came in with him, Mrs. B."

Daily Express, February 12th, 1959

A constable may soon arrest without warrant anyone whom he believes to be carrying an offensive weapon; an offensive weapon is defined as "any article made or adapted to cause injury, or intended by the person having it for such use."

Sunday Express, February 15th, 1953

"Your turn will come when Daddy finds out you sent them all."

Sunday Express, February 15th, 1976

"If Cruft's gave an award for the best retriever on my estate, we know who'd
be supreme champion, eh, Dodger?"

Sunday Express, February 15th, 1981

"You can relax now Vera – they've caught the wolf and denied the escaped puma story."

Daily Express, February 16th, 1965

"Goody, goody, our getaway car – what kept yer, Percy?"

Sunday Express, February 18th, 1979

"Do you want to end up as a Guardsman's hat outside Buckingham Palace?"

Sunday Express, February 22nd, 1959

"One day return Waterloo, please."

Daily Express, February 23rd, 1976

"And to think we stop people coming into the country because they've got a few undesirable friends."

Daily Express, February 28th, 1967

"Watch him, Harry – he'll still be a bit hungry."
(Britain had a week revelling with Goldie, a Golden Eagle who escaped from London Zoo.)

Sunday Express, March 7th, 1965

"Don't disturb Butch – he's calling that little Jack Russell who answers telephones."
(Dog answers phone when owner's out.)

Daily Express, March 10th, 1983

"I'll give you 'To err is human; to forgive divine,' my boy."
(Goldie returned home.)

Daily Express, March 11th, 1965

"For allowing your car to be left 3 minutes beyond the allotted time on a yellow line twice in one year there is no punishment too severe. It is therefore my duty…"

Daily Express, March 19th, 1970

QUOTE: "A man can show his wife that he loves her in a thousand ways without saying it.
He can show it by his look of pleasure on seeing her." ("Getting Married," by B.M.A., 2s.)

Daily Express, March 21st, 1967

"Hey ho, first day of spring – all those who haven't got Asian flu have got gastro-enteritis."

Daily Express, March 21st, 1963

"Here come three of my good reasons for bringing back hanging."

Sunday Express, March 21st, 1982

"I don't care if you are sick of photographing weddings – you've no right to punch my Alfie's nose."

Sunday Express, March 22nd, 1959

It's always an Easter BRIDE we hear about, preparing for her wedding.
Here we have an Easter BRIDEGROOM preparing for his.

Daily Express, March 27th, 1953

"Watch out for the wild swings to the body, the swift uppercuts – her horse fell at the first fence and her team got knocked out of the semi-finals."

Sunday Express, March 28th, 1965

"That takes care of the Canal Turn, now for Becher's."

Daily Express, March 30th, 1967

"Achtung! A car!"

Daily Express, March 31st, 1970

"I've made a mental note for Whitsun of all the ones who snowballed me at Easter."

Daily Express, April 1st, 1975

"Joke cigars for April Fool's Day prompt me to suggest you're long overdue retirement, Hennesey."

Daily Express, April 1st, 1980

"Hurry up, Bertie – you'll be late for the match."

Daily Express, April 4th, 1967

"Finish making Grandma's Easter egg later and tell her breakfast is ready."

Sunday Express, April 6th, 1980

"I try my hardest to like the Labour Government and then they do things like this…"

Daily Express, April 8th, 1976

"Hold it! If we're entering a team and I'm in charge of you, you're wearing these."

Sunday Express, April 17th, 1983

"I hope this client knows what he's doing – giving us a bob for every pylon we knock down on his farm."

Sunday Express, April 18th, 1965

"Oh dear, now we really are on the brink of World War 3 – he's out first ball of the season."

Sunday Express, April 27th, 1980

"A plague on their 'One more race round the lightship'. And a plague on the Royal Society of Health for saying the swinging life begins at 50."

Sunday Express, April 30th, 1967

"You look after his missus – I'll handle him."

Sunday Express, May 2nd, 1965

Fascinating item from a National newspaper, last week: "With intelligent use of space and modern methods of blending highways into the scenery, the beauties of the countryside will always be preserved." Wanna bet?

Sunday Express, May 3rd, 1964

"So far she hasn't joined the chorus of witty jokes about inflation."

Sunday Express, May 18th, 1980

"Miss!"

Sunday Express, May 19th, 1963

"Watch out for the one next door – it bites."

Daily Express, May 19th, 1970

"I knew it! Letting 'em play cricket at Lord's was the thin edge of the wedge."

Daily Express, May 20th, 1976

"One of them started a rumour it had leaked out they were going
to make her a Dame in the new Honours List."

Sunday Express, May 23rd, 1976

"Nice i'nt it – making us drink out here just because she's got a new bit of carpet in the bar."

Daily Express, May 24th, 1965

"If I was Mrs Thatcher and had to choose between cleaning up the Middle East or cleaning up dirty Britain I'd choose the Middle East."

Daily Express, May 29th, 1986

"Now who's going to tell him Uncle Ernie and Auntie Rosie and the children are coming to tea?"

Sunday Express, May 31st, 1970

"This will cheer you up – the Scout gives the same odds for you being in the first ten as he gives Ken Livingstone being Home Secretary in a Thatcher Government."

Daily Express, May 31st, 1983

"Well, I don't think this is better than spending the week-end in Aunt Rosie's stuffy front room."

Sunday Express, June 2nd, 1963

"That's how the Aussies do it – bowl 'em on the feet, make 'em hop out of their crease, and BINGO!!"

Daily Express, June 13th, 1975

"That Spanish ticket fella who told us to 'Wait in here a minute…'"

Sunday Express, June 13th, 1982

"I thought I told you to get down and hide the TV programmes before your father saw them."

Sunday Express, June 20th, 1965

"It is the easiest thing in the world for a child to detect that you're not really listening to him."…Marriage Guidance Council.

Daily Express, June 20th, 1969

"That's your father – always looking on the bright side – 'Do we realise that from today the nights start drawing in and we'll soon be thinking about Christmas cards.'"

Sunday Express, June 21st, 1964

"What do you mean – 'On your feet, everyone or we'll be late for the game!' We arranged this picnic before we even knew they'd be playing."

Sunday Express, June 22nd, 1986

En garde!

A telephone service enabling callers to see as well as speak to each other has started today in New York, Washington, and Chicago. It was inaugurated by Mrs. Lindon Johnson, wife of the president.

"Switch the lights out, fellers, while I phone my missus to tell her I'm working late at the office."

Daily Express, June 26th, 1964

"Will you tell your blasted kids not to keep phoning me in the bath!"

"Whadya know! Old Mrs. Humberg wears one of those topless affairs around the house."

"I can't come tonight Hughie—Mummy wants me to stay home and help her with the ironing."

"I wouldn't say we can't come as Fred's in bed with a nasty cold if he wasn't, would I?"

"It's your Mother, darling."

Daily Express, June 26th, 1964

"I know as a miners' M.P. I've got to do everything Mr. Scargill tells me but I'm damn sure it doesn't include looking after your kids and doing your wife's shopping."

Daily Express, June 29th, 1975

"Too much sitting on their backsides watching Wimbledon, that's their trouble."

Sunday Express, July 5th, 1981

"I don't fancy your chances of survival if he comes round."

Daily Express, July 6th, 1967

"The children are back – they've videoed the whole sixteen hours of yesterday's Rock Concert in case you missed it."

Sunday Express, July 14th, 1985

"I did what you told me, dear – walked straight up the platform and took a bang at the driver."
(During the railway 'go-slow' battles broke out between drivers and passengers.)

Daily Express, July 15th, 1965

"Here we are, Einstein – a field in which you cannot fail to shine."

Daily Express, July 15th, 1975

"I told him we wouldn't sing unless he paid us the same as St. Paul's Choir and all he said was 'Thanks'."

Sunday Express, July 19th, 1981

"There are some of us who look on the absence of 'planes with utter joy – old boy."

Sunday Express, July 30th, 1978

"That man we paid £10 a head to take us across – I suppose this is his boat?"

Sunday Express, August 1st, 1982

"Better positions for Wardens…" (Civil Service Union)

Daily Express, August 7th, 1969

"And what's this item – To losses sustained at poker while servicing my car?"

Daily Express, August 10th, 1967

"How come coppers never go on strike when they put in a wage claim?"

Daily Express, August 12th, 1965

"If I was your Fred with an appointment on Monday about his contract
I wouldn't have clobbered the Chairman first ball."

Sunday Express, August 16th, 1981

"I haven't the heart to tell them their Tibby's had six lovely little kittens."

Daily Express, August 21st, 1980

"I know the Chief doesn't like the police bending the law, but I don't suppose he'd mind us bending it just this once."

Daily Express, August 22nd, 1978

"Worst case of keeping up with the Joneses I've seen for a long time."
(Council house tenant opens garden to public – headline.)

Daily Express, August 22nd, 1967

"If he's right, some of your flock will end up as roast lamb."

Sunday Express, August 22nd, 1982

"Leave him be, Arthur – it's not his fault your team paid £600,000 for a right-winger and lost 8-0."

Sunday Express, August 25th, 1963

"My wife says if Mrs Thatcher can be in and out of hospital in one day and back to work the next, so can I."

Daily Express, August 26th, 1982